SPANISH COOKING
for Beginners

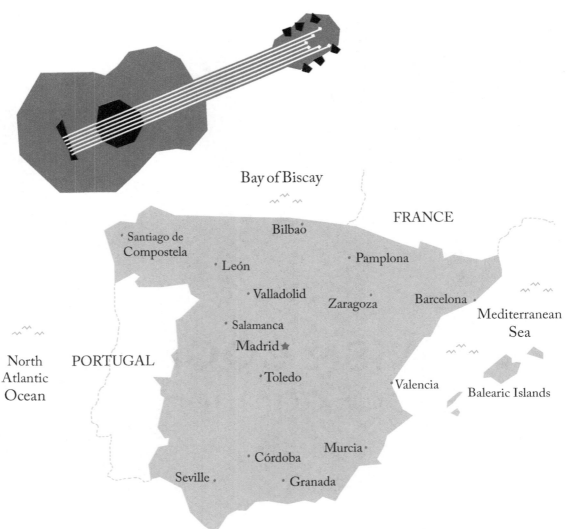

Bay of Biscay

FRANCE

Santiago de
Compostela

Bilbao

León

Pamplona

Valladolid

Zaragoza

Barcelona

Salamanca

Mediterranean
Sea

North
Atlantic
Ocean

PORTUGAL

Madrid ★

Toledo

Valencia

Balearic Islands

Córdoba

Murcia

Seville

Granada

Canary Islands

SPANISH COOKING
for Beginners

GABRIELA LLAMAS

Simple and
Delicious
Recipes
for All
Occasions

NEW SHOE PRESS

© 2022 Quarto Publishing Group USA Inc.
Text © 2016 Quarto Publishing Group USA Inc.

First Published in 2022 by New Shoe Press, an imprint of The Quarto Group, 100 Cummings Center, Suite 265-D, Beverly, MA 01915, USA.
T (978) 282-9590 F (978) 283-2742 Quarto.com

New Shoe Press titles are also available at discount for retail, wholesale, promotional, and bulk purchase. For details, contact the Special Sales Manager by email at specialsales@quarto.com or by mail at The Quarto Group, Attn: Special Sales Manager, 100 Cummings Center, Suite 265-D, Beverly, MA 01915, USA.

ISBN: 978-0-7603-7958-5
eISBN: 978-0-7603-7959-2

The content in this book was previously published in *Let's Cook Spanish: A Family Cookbook* (Quarry Books 2016) by Gabriela Llamas.

Library of Congress Cataloging-in-Publication Data available

Illustrations: Laia Albaladejo
Photography: Shutterstock
Editorial assistance: Susana Lopez Ruesga

Dedication

Thank you to my amazing children:
Enrique, Primi, and Sofia. I am very
proud of their intelligence and of
their great heart.

Contents

Introduction

In Spain we love to share our food and its preparation with family and friends in a fun and festive atmosphere. Looking at the history of Spain, we see a country that is a crossroads for people from different parts of the world. Spanish food integrates the cooking of Phoenicians, Greeks, Romans, Visigoths, Arabs, French, and English, as well as foods and spices from the Americas.

Food and cooking supports communication at different levels with creativity, independence, responsibility, order, motivation, concentration, patience, and courage. It also encourages manual skills and teaches biology, language, math, mythology, history, art, and geography—as well as a sense of beauty, harmony, and order. It shows us how to love not only by being present but also by letting the children play a part—something which sometimes seems impossible!

This exposure enriches our food culture. Many of the recipes you will find in this book are a tale, a myth, a discovery, and an adventure. They are a return to our fascinating origins which today we can still enjoy with our senses and which we want to share with you.

Tapas and Pinchos

Tapas and pinchos are small bites of fresh, delicious food to be eaten with drinks—anything from a few olives or almonds to a small serving of a more elaborate dish. Nobody knows their origin. Maybe they came from a decree of King Alfonso the Wise who ordered that no wine would be served at the inns in Castille unless accompanied by something to eat. It is also attributed to the taverns in Andalucía: A piece of bread or ham a tapa (lid) prevented flies and insects from falling in the wine. It is a casual, relaxed, and happy style of eating in company. It means sociability, fun, friendship, and generosity. It is a way of living—and such an important part of our culture that we even have a verb for it: "tapear" (to eat tapas). With simple, healthy ingredients we have developed incredibly creative ways to turn our food into something extremely attractive.

Bread with Olive Oil, Tomato, and Iberian Ham

SERVES 4

Iberian pigs, called "olives with legs," are our unique and special ingredient because they have a high nutritional value and live in a specific ecosystem, the Dehesa, found only in a small part of Spain in the areas around Salamanca, Extremadura, Andalucía, and on the border with Portugal. Prairies with holm oaks supply these free-range animals with grass and acorns, which are rich in oleic acid, the same component found in olive oil. This dish is best made with freshly baked bread.

1 ripe tomato

4 slices good-quality bread

2 tablespoons (30 ml) extra-virgin olive oil

4 slices Ibérico or Serrano ham

1 garlic clove (with skin on) cut in half (optional)

Cut the tomato in half across the width, not from the stem, and grate with a coarse vegetable grater. Be careful with your fingers! Discard the leftover tomato skin.

Drizzle the bread with olive oil, spread with grated tomato (not too much), and put a slice of ham on top. If you choose to add garlic, do so by rubbing it on the bread before adding olive oil or tomato.

You may lightly toast the bread, but do not let it become hard. We often have bread, tomato, and olive oil for breakfast. A little Iberian ham adds high-quality protein.

NOTE

Bread, olive oil, and tomato go with everything including fish, meats, vegetables, and cheese. Make a sauce by mixing tomato, olive oil, salt, and mashed garlic. Place the bread and some spoons around for everyone to help themselves. Be sure to make plenty!

Basic Potato Omelet

SERVES 4

In Spain, the potato omelet is the typical mid-morning tapa. When I was a kid, we used to have it for dinner accompanied by a tomato and tuna salad. You can personalize this dish by adding fried chorizo or other type of sausage or by adding other vegetables. The recipe requires your parents' help because it involves very hot oil.

1 cup (240 ml) extra-virgin olive oil

1 pound (500 g) Ratte, Yukon Gold, or other good-quality potato

1 medium (140 g) onion, peeled and sliced

4 large, organic eggs

½ teaspoon salt

8-inch (20 cm) omelet pan (with flat handle)

A plate larger than the pan

Put olive oil in the pan. Add the onion. Peel potatoes and slice thinly using a knife or mandoline. Place the potatoes in the pan. Add half the salt and place the pan over high heat.

When the oil starts bubbling around the edges of the pan, lower the heat to medium-low, cover, and let potatoes cook for approximately 15 to 20 minutes. Stir occasionally so that they cook evenly. They should be soft but not browned. They should not lose their shape. Drain in a colander, and reserve the olive oil.

Crack the eggs in a bowl, add the remaining salt, and beat thoroughly. Add the potatoes and mix gently. Put the pan over heat with 1½ tablespoons (23 ml) of olive oil and, when very hot, add the egg-potato mixture. It is very important that the pan be sizzling hot. Cook for 2 minutes over high heat and turn the omelet over.

To turn the omelet over: Use a kitchen glove so you do not burn your hand. Place the plate firmly over the pan and your gloved hand over the plate. Take the handle of the pan with the other hand. With a quick movement, flip the contents of the pan onto the plate. Return the pan to the heat, add one tablespoon (15 ml) of olive oil, and slide the uncooked side of the omelet back into the pan. Cook for another 2 minutes, shaking the pan to prevent sticking. Lower the heat and cook for another 1 or 2 minutes to the consistency you prefer. We like our omelets a little runny.

Stuffed potato omelet:
If for any reason the omelet is too dry, you can stuff your omelet as they do in the North of Spain or add a sauce to it to give it juiciness. Split the omelet in half. Spread each half with mayonnaise, and then add lettuce and tomato. Then place the omelet together. Slice into 8 portions or triangles and place each over a piece of toast and garnish with an olive, a cherry tomato, or more mayonnaise to taste.

Mushrooms with Garlic Parsley Sauce in the Style of La Rioja

MAKES 6 SKEWERS

These pinchos are messy to eat, but that is part of the fun. Some people prefer to remove the skewer and arrange the mushroom and the shrimp on top of the bread. Soriano, a family bar on Logroño's Laurel Street, is packed with customers eating this pincho. Their family recipe is a closely guarded secret. I have often enjoyed tapas here with my friend Judith from La Rioja, and I have created my own version of this pincho.

1 clove garlic, peeled

1 tablespoon (4 g) packed chopped parsley

5 tablespoons (75 ml) extra-virgin olive oil, divided

2 tablespoons (30 ml) lemon juice

18 large mushrooms

Salt and freshly ground pepper

6 small shrimp, peeled

6 wooden skewers

6 slices bread

Combine the garlic, parsley, 4 tablespoons (60 ml) of the olive oil, lemon juice, and salt in a blender until it is a green sauce. Set aside.

Clean the mushrooms with a soft brush and remove the stems. Put the remaining 1 tablespoon (15 ml) olive oil in a pan that can fit all the mushroom caps.

Heat the pan, and when the oil is hot, add the mushrooms, stem-side down. Sprinkle with salt and pepper, and cook for 2 to 3 minutes over medium heat. When they begin to brown, turn over, and add the shrimp with a little more salt and pepper. Cook for 2 to 3 minutes, drizzling some of the garlic parsley sauce over each mushroom. Remember to cook the shrimp on both sides.

Pierce 1 shrimp and 3 mushrooms on each skewer. Add a slice of bread and place on a serving platter. Continue with the remaining shrimp and mushrooms until finished. Drizzle with a little more garlic parsley sauce.

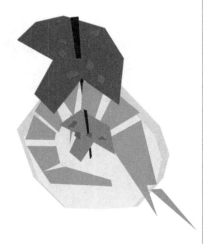

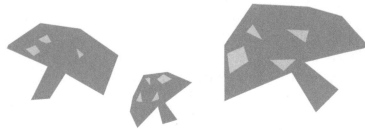

Pickled Tuna Fish

SERVES 4 TO 6

In hot climates, pickling in vinegar is a traditional way to preserve food. Any fish can be used but it works better with blue fish such as sardines, tuna, and mackerel. There are many slight variations in the pickling of vegetables and spices, but olive oil and vinegar are essential. Pickles are best made in earthenware pots because they do not react to vinegar.

2¼ pounds (1 kg) tuna fish

1 cup (235 ml) extra-virgin olive oil, divided

1 head garlic

1 large onion, sliced

½ cup (120 ml) dry white wine

1 cup (235 ml) sherry vinegar

½ cup (120 ml) apple cider vinegar

2 cups (470 ml) water

10 peppercorns

4 bay leaves

1 whole garlic clove

1 teaspoon dried thyme or a few sprigs fresh thyme

1 teaspoon salt

½ teaspoon sugar

Wash the fish thoroughly and pat dry. Cut into thick chunks or slices of approximately 1 inch (2.5 cm).

Put 2 tablespoons (30 ml) of the olive oil in a pan and sear the tuna on all sides until golden. Set aside. (You may also steam the fish if you prefer.)

Peel the garlic cloves. Using an enamel pot, heat the remaining oil, and fry the onion and garlic for 3 minutes. Add the wine, both vinegars, water, peppercorns, bay leaves, garlic clove, thyme, salt, and sugar, bringing to a boil. Boil for 6 to 8 minutes. Reduce the heat to low.

Add the fish to the escabeche liquid and cook for 1 to 2 minutes over very gentle heat.

Turn the heat off and allow to cool to room temperature. Once cool, transfer to a glass or earthenware bowl (do not store in a metal or plastic container) and keep in the refrigerator. The fish must be completely covered with liquid. If more liquid is needed, boil 2 cups (470 ml) water with ¼ cup (60 ml) vinegar for 5 minutes and add to the fish. Wait for 3 days before eating. It will keep for at least a month.

The pickled fish can be used for many different recipes such as salads, patties, stuffed vegetables, and all kinds of tapas.

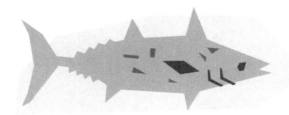

Stuffed Eggs

SERVES 4

Eggs are a great revitalizing food. In addition to being a good source of protein, in Spain they also have a symbolic significance representing renewal and fertility. For example, we use them as decorations during Easter time in sweet cakes, such as monas, where they are placed whole and raw in their shells, on top of the batter just before baking. They make simple and beautiful decorations.

4 hard-boiled eggs, peeled and cut in half

½ cup (120 g) Pickled Tuna Fish (page 22)

½ cup (120 g) mayonnaise

1 tablespoon (4 g) minced fresh parsley or chives

8 olives

8 large shrimp, peeled and cooked

8 wooden skewers

Minced parsley, for garnish

Remove 2 egg yolks and set aside.

Combine the tuna fish, mayonnaise, 2 remaining egg yolks, and minced parsley in a bowl. Cut off a small slice of the bottom of the egg white to help the egg stay in place. Stuff the eggs with this mixture and place on a serving platter.

Skewer an olive and a shrimp on each skewer and stick on each stuffed egg.

Garnish with the minced parsley. Place the reserved egg yolks in a colander, press with a big spoon. The egg yolk decoration dries out quickly, so it should be made just before serving.

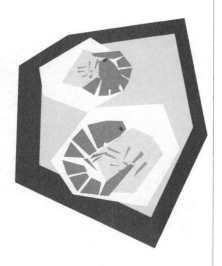

Monkfish and Shrimp Salad

SERVES 4 AS A MAIN

Salpicón is a cold dish prepared with cooked ingredients such as seafood or chicken, diced or shredded, and seasoned with vinaigrette. Originally made with cheap cuts of meat and considered a humble dish, salpicón today is known as a fish dish. It can be served as a tapa, an appetizer, or a healthy main dish. Make it your own by mixing in different seafood, such as mussels or squid. Just remember to cook them first. In some parts of Spain, minced, hard-boiled egg is added as well.

½ tablespoon (9 g) salt

1 bay leaf

2 or 3 monkfish fillets (about 20 ounces, or 560 g), cleaned and deboned

1 red bell pepper, seeded and finely diced

1 green Italian pepper, seeded and finely diced

1 small onion, diced

1 almost green mango, peeled, pitted, and finely diced

3 tablespoons (36 g) minced pickled cucumber

¾ cup (180 ml) extra-virgin olive oil, Arbequina variety if possible

¼ cup (60 ml) sherry vinegar

¼ cup (60 ml) apple cider vinegar

Juice of 1 lemon

12 jumbo prawns, cooked, peeled, and cut in half

3 cups (about 10 ounces, or 280 g) small shrimp or prawns, cooked and peeled

1 tablespoon (4 g) minced fresh parsley

Diced avocado, other fish or seafood such as tuna, hake, mussels, octopus, or clams (optional)

Garnish

Lettuce leaves and toast

NOTE

The addition of mango and pickled cucumber is not traditional, but we really love it at home. Sometimes we add diced avocado, yellow bell pepper, and even corn.

Heat water in a saucepan, add salt, the bay leaf, and the monkfish fillets and bring to a boil. Lower the heat and cook for 5 to 8 minutes. This will depend on the size of the fish. Turn the heat off, strain, and set aside. (You may also grill the fish.)

In a glass or ceramic bowl, combine the peppers, onion, mango, cucumber, extra-virgin olive oil, both vinegars, lemon juice, and salt. Mix well. Add the shrimp or prawns.

Peel the monkfish if there is any skin left, and cut into chunks the size of a cherry tomato or a little larger. Add to the bowl and mix gently. Garnish with the minced parsley.

Refrigerate or serve at room temperature. As a tapa, put a lettuce leaf over toast and scoop some salpicón on top.

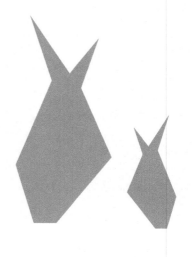

Grilled Green Asparagus with Orange Mayonnaise

SERVES 4

Did you know that green and white asparagus are the same beautiful plant? White asparagus are covered with earth as soon as they begin to poke through. They never see the sunlight. Green asparagus are allowed to grow out of the earth and catch the sun's rays, therefore generating green chlorophyll. I grow them in my orchard and they are great fun to pick. You will find this is a very popular vegetable tapa.

16 green asparagus (discard the hard bottom)

2 tablespoons (30 ml) extra-virgin olive oil, divided

Salt

Orange mayonnaise

2 tablespoons (30 ml) fresh orange juice

⅛ teaspoon (a small pinch) powdered saffron

1 tablespoon (15 ml) lemon juice

1 teaspoon grated fresh organic orange peel

1 cup (240 g) mayonnaise

Salt and freshly ground pepper

Garnish

Fried almonds

Cured Manchego cheese, thinly sliced

Hold the asparagus with both hands and break off the hard bottom part. If they do not break easily, try a bit higher on the stalk. Cut the base with a knife to even the break. Clean them and allow to dry.

Place a cast-iron pan over high heat, add 1 tablespoon (15 ml) of the olive oil, sprinkle some salt all over the pan, and place the asparagus on top. Grill for 3 to 4 minutes, and then turn over. Add the remaining 1 tablespoon (15 ml) olive oil, a sprinkle of salt, and grill for a few more minutes. They must retain their green color and remain a little crunchy.

To make the orange mayonnaise: Heat the orange juice in a small pan over medium heat, and when hot, add the saffron. Place in a bowl. Add the lemon juice, grated orange peel, and mayonnaise. Season with salt and pepper. Mix well.

Serve the asparagus from the grill with a bowl of sauce and some extra salt and pepper over them. You may also garnish with some minced fried almonds or thinly sliced, cured Manchego cheese.

NOTE

If you want to cook this dish on the barbecue, it is easier to spread olive oil on the asparagus before placing on the grill. Asparagus should be salted after grilling.

Salad My Way

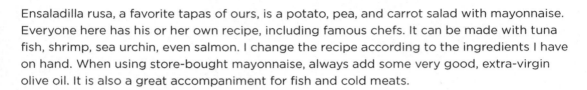

SERVES 4 AS A MAIN DISH

Ensaladilla rusa, a favorite tapas of ours, is a potato, pea, and carrot salad with mayonnaise. Everyone here has his or her own recipe, including famous chefs. It can be made with tuna fish, shrimp, sea urchin, even salmon. I change the recipe according to the ingredients I have on hand. When using store-bought mayonnaise, always add some very good, extra-virgin olive oil. It is also a great accompaniment for fish and cold meats.

¾ cup (100 g) peeled and diced green beans

2 carrots, peeled and diced

¾ cup (100 g) fresh shelled peas (frozen will do)

8 green asparagus, (discard the hard bottom) sliced

3 cups (500 g) peeled, diced potatoes, celeriac bulb, or chayote (vegetable pear)

1 cup (240 g) mayonnaise

½ cup (120 g) yogurt

¼ cup (60 ml) extra-virgin olive oil

1 teaspoon anchovy paste

1 tablespoon (15 ml) lemon juice

1 teaspoon grated organic lemon peel

Minced chives

Salt and freshly ground pepper

Cook the green beans in abundantly salted boiling water for 4 minutes. Drain to another pan and place the beans in a bowl. Cook the carrots and peas in the same salted water for 3 minutes, then drain and add to the bowl. Cook the asparagus in the same water for 1 minute, then drain and add it to the bowl. Finally, add the potatoes and cook for 4 to 5 minutes, depending on the size of the chunks. Drain and place in the bowl.

In a separate bowl, mix together the mayonnaise, yogurt, olive oil, anchovy paste, lemon juice, grated peel, chives, salt and pepper. Pour over the vegetables and mix carefully.

This is a great classic with many uses in the tapas world. You may serve it on toast or in small bowls with a garnish of your choice, such as cooked shrimp, pickled tuna, anchovies, olives, roasted red pepper, capers, beetroot, or pickled cucumber. You can also roll it in a slice of smoked salmon and put it on top of bread.

NOTE

If you do not eat dairy, you can make a dressing with tofu, soy creamer, olive oil, lemon, vinegar, chives, and yellow miso paste.

Roasted Vegetables on Toast

MAKES 24 TO 30 TAPAS

We have a great tradition of roasting potatoes, garlic, pumpkin, chestnuts, and sweet potatoes over hot coals. It comes from our very wise and humble popular country cuisine, which uses fire as a cooking method. This is more of a late summer/early autumn dish, when peppers, tomatoes, eggplants, and onions are at their best. It is very popular in the area of Aragón, Valencia, and Barcelona. Try roasting a whole garlic head and a few raw almonds, and then mash and mix with extra-virgin olive oil and salt as a substitute for the olive sauce.

Olive sauce

1 cup (150 g) black pitted olives

½ cup (120 ml) extra-virgin olive oil

½ clove garlic

½ teaspoon thyme

1 tablespoon (4 g) chopped fresh parsley

1 teaspoon lemon juice

2 tablespoons (30 ml) water

Freshly ground pepper

Vegetables

2 onions

2 red bell peppers

2 tomatoes

2 eggplants

Olive oil

Salt

24 to 30 slices sourdough bread

Garnish

Alcaparrones (large pickled capers)

Anchovies in olive oil (½ or 1 per toast)

Slices of goat cheese

Basil leaves

Pickled Tuna Fish (page 22)

Thinly sliced cecina (dry-cured meat)

Extra-virgin olive oil, Picual variety or other good brand

3 tablespoons (12 g) minced parsley

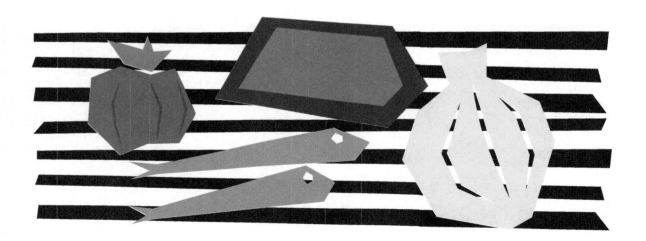

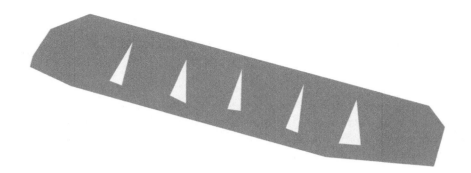

Preheat the oven to 425°F (220°C or gas mark 7).

To make the sauce: Wash the olives in cold water, place in a blender, and add the rest of the ingredients. Process until smooth and set aside.

To roast your vegetables on the barbecue: Cut the onions, peppers, tomatoes, and eggplant in half to shorten cooking time and drizzle with a little olive oil. The skin gets charred and the vegetables have a smoky aroma, which adds to the flavor. Peel the vegetables while still warm (it will be easier).

On a slice of bread, spread a teaspoon of olive sauce, place a piece of each vegetable, add any of the garnishes, drizzle with extra-virgin olive oil, and add a little minced parsley.

NOTE

You may also toss the roasted vegetables in the olive sauce, add greens or cooked pasta, and make a delicious salad!

Barbecued Shrimp in Garlic Sauce

MAKES 30 SKEWERS

This traditional tapa from central and southern Spain is best made with fresh, whole shrimp. Peel the shrimp and set aside the heads and shell for fish stock. Cook with sliced garlic and some dried chile pepper in a generous amount of extra-virgin olive oil and serve sizzling hot from its earthenware casserole. The resulting oily sauce is delicious for dipping bread! This is adapted for a barbecue; be careful not to overcook the shrimp.

1 cup (235 ml) extra-virgin olive oil

1½ cups (90 g) loosely packed parsley leaves

4 to 6 cloves garlic, peeled

1½ red bird's eye chile peppers, stemmed but not seeded

1 teaspoon salt

2¼ pounds (1 kg) peeled jumbo shrimp

30 wooden skewers, soaked in water for 30 minutes

In a blender, combine the olive oil, parsley, garlic, chile peppers, and salt. Blend until you obtain a smooth green sauce with little red bits. Pour into a large bowl. Add shrimp to the bowl with the sauce and marinate for 10 minutes.

Place 3 shrimp on each skewer. Do not press each shrimp too close to each other or the center one will not cook properly. Spread a little marinade on the shrimp and grill over high heat for 1 minute on each side. You may cook this directly on the barbecue or in a skillet.

While one side is cooking, add more marinade before turning over. Feel free to adapt the amount of garlic and chile pepper to suit your taste. We like them very garlicky.

Serve as they come off the grill. A small glass of cold gazpacho or salmorejo is a refreshing contrast. Place a bowl of lemon mayonnaise on the table for those who wish to dip.

Vegetable Cocas

SERVES 6 TO 8

Peppers were first introduced to Spain by the explorer Christopher Columbus. In Spain, the farming of peppers is now associated with the monasteries of San Pedro de Ñora in Murcia, and San Jerónimo de Yuste in Extremadura, the retirement place of Emperor Charles the Fifth. Both areas are still producing excellent pimentón (paprika), but Yuste's is well known for its smoky flavor. This is because in this region the climate is more humid and the peppers are dried with oak wood.

3 tablespoons (45 ml) extra-virgin olive oil

2 onions, minced

2 pounds (1 kg) spinach and Swiss chard leaves

¼ teaspoon salt

Freshly ground pepper

Dough

½ cup (120 ml) warm water

½ cup (120 ml) extra-virgin olive oil

1 teaspoon salt

½ teaspoon sugar

1 teaspoon dry yeast

3 cups (240 g) all-purpose flour

1 teaspoon Pimentón de la Vera (sweet, smoky paprika)

¼ cup (65 g) raisins (soak in water for 1 to 2 hours)

4 tablespoons (40 g) pine nuts

Preheat the oven to 425° F (220° C or gas mark 7).

Sauté the olive oil, onion, and salt over medium heat for 3 to 4 minutes. Add spinach and Swiss chard leaves and sauté over high heat for 10 more minutes. Season with pepper and drain in a colander. Set aside. (If vegetables are not drained properly, they will spoil the dough.)

To make the dough: In a bowl, combine water, olive oil, salt, sugar, and yeast. Stir well and add the flour. (This process can be done by machine.) Knead for 1 to 2 minutes, until the dough is very soft and not sticky. If it is too hard, add oil and water in the same proportion simultaneously, until you reach the desired consistency.

Roll the dough out on a parchment paper into a 12 x 24-inch (30 x 60 cm) thin rectangle. Transfer to a baking tray. Distribute the drained vegetables on top of the dough, spread evenly, and then sprinkle with pimentón (paprika), drained raisins, and pine nuts. Bake in the center of the oven for 15 to 20 minutes, or until the edges turn golden.

Serve hot or warm.

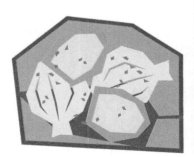

NOTE

Cocas are our local pizza. There is a great variety of them. You may use different vegetables, add cheese if you like, and make them your own.

PIMENTÓN PICANTE

PIM
AH

Meat and Fish

We are very fond of what we call spoon dishes: stews, hot pots, pulses, cereal, and soups—anything where bread can be included. But in Spain we also like fish and seafood of which we have an excellent variety—so fresh we like them cooked simply. A children's favorite is hake with green sauce.

My family loves the gravy of the meat. The children dip pieces of bread we call barquitos (little boats) in it. Here you will find a few of our favorite easy classics. Feel free to increase ingredients to make more sauce!

Valencian Paella

SERVES 4

This is a very traditional dish from the Spanish area of Levante by the Mediterranean Sea. It is often cooked in the open air over a wood fire with controlled heat. Ingredients are sautéed in the center of the paella, a flat. round pan which lends its name to the dish. When ingredients are cooked to the desired state, they are pushed to the sides of the pan in order to allow room for the next batch.

½ cup (120 ml) extra-virgin olive oil

1½ pounds (600 g) organic, free-range, skinless chicken, cut into small 1 to 1½-inch (3 cm) pieces

¾ pound (340 g) rabbit cut in small pieces (You can substitute with more chicken or ½ pound (200 g) diced pork.)

1 green or red bell pepper, seeded and sliced

½ pound (250 g) green beans cut into 3 pieces each

1 jar (10½ ounces, or 300 g) artichoke hearts, or 6 fresh artichoke hearts, cut into 4 pieces each

3 garlic cloves, minced

¾ pound (340 g) tomatoes, grated or peeled, finely chopped

¼ pound (100 g) dry, large, flat white bean (Garrofó variety or any other white bean) Soak in water a day ahead and then cook for 1 hour covered in water. Reserve the cooking liquid for chicken stock.

¾ pound (400 g) rice, Bomba variety or Calasparra

1 tablespoon (7 g) pimentón (paprika)

¼ teaspoon saffron threads or saffron powder

6 cups (1.5 L) chicken stock

12 cooked snails, optional

1 rosemary sprig

Put about ¼ cup (60 ml) of olive oil in an 18-inch (45 cm) paella pan, and add salt to prevent splattering. Sauté each of the meats over gentle heat for about 15 to 20 minutes. Meanwhile, heat the chicken stock with the rosemary sprig to the boiling point and then add the saffron. Keep warm.

Transfer the meat pieces to the edge of the pan when cooked. Add a little more olive oil and sauté the peppers, green beans, and artichoke hearts for 5 to 8 minutes. Place on the sides of the pan and then add the garlic and tomato, and stir fry until the liquid has evaporated. Add more olive oil and fry the rice for 1 to 2 minutes. Add pimentón and stir for a few seconds. Then add the hot chicken stock (1 L or 4 cups) and raise the heat until it boils. Stir in the rice, and then add the fava beans. Cook for 10 minutes over high heat, and then lower the heat and cook until the rice is nearly tender, another 8 to 10 minutes. Turn the heat off, cover with a lid, and wait for 5 minutes to allow the rice to cook completely. Add the snails to warm through, if using. The rice should be dry, loose, and cooked, but still firm in the center.

The rice proportions are 1 portion of rice to 2 to 2½ portions of stock, but more liquid may be needed if the heat is high and too much evaporation occurs.

Shrimp Fideuá or Pasta Paella

SERVES 4

Fideuá originated in Gandía on the coast of Levante. The name comes from fideos, or short, thin noodles. This is our homemade recipe. I made it on a day when my children invited many of their friends home and all the markets were closed. I had no fish, just a few shrimp, and other leftovers. It has now become one of our favorite dishes. If you cannot find short noodles, just break up some spaghetti. Any other kind of short pasta will do; just adapt the amount of liquid and the cooking time.

⅔ cup (160 ml) extra-virgin olive oil, more as needed

⅔ cup (100 g) diced fennel bulb

1 onion, diced

1 cup (140 g) diced red bell pepper

2 teaspoons (12 g) salt, divided

2 ripe tomatoes, grated

4 cloves garlic, minced

1½ cups (300 g) medium-size or large shrimp, peeled

2¼ cups (400 g) fideuá pasta; short, hollow, round, half-moon noodles; or any other short, thin pasta

2 teaspoons (5 g) sweet pimentón de la Vera or paprika

4 cups (940 ml) hot fish stock, vegetable stock, or water

½ cup (75 g) shelled fresh peas

⅛ teaspoon powdered saffron or a pinch saffron threads

16-inch (40 cm) paella pan

Add the olive oil, fennel, onion, bell pepper, and 1 teaspoon (3 g) of the salt to the paella pan and sauté for 10 to 12 minutes, or until the vegetables are well cooked and start to turn golden.

Add the grated tomato and garlic and fry until the water has evaporated.

Add the shrimp and fry for 1 minute, then add the pasta and fry for 1 to 2 more minutes. All should be well coated with olive oil; if necessary, add a little more oil.

Add the pimentón (or paprika) and stir gently; do not allow the pimentón to burn or it will become bitter.

Immediately add the hot stock, peas, saffron, and remaining 1 teaspoon (3 g) salt and mix well to distribute the ingredients. If some of the mixture sticks to the pan, just scrape and stir; it will add flavor to the dish. Bring to a boil and cook over high heat for 6 to 9 minutes, or as directed on the pasta package. If necessary, lower the heat or add more liquid.

You may cook it until it is very dry or leave a bit juicy, but always serve the pasta al dente. Let rest for 3 to 5 minutes before serving.

NOTE

The general rule is 1 part pasta to 2 parts liquid, but this varies with the type of pasta.

Homemade Meatballs

SERVES 4

Meatballs can be made with different kinds of meat or bread, as well as parsley and seasonings according to your taste. You can add pitted green olives, baby mushrooms, or peas to the sauce. In some parts of Spain, they are cooked with squid. Just remember to add your extra ingredients when you pour the sauce over so that they cook together.

¾ ounce (20 g) hard bread or 1¾ ounces (50 g) fresh bread crumbs

¼ cup (60 ml) milk

¾ cup (120 g) minced fried onion, divided

1 small egg

3 tablespoons (12 g) minced parsley, divided, plus more for garnish

Salt and freshly ground pepper

1⅓ pounds (600 g) freshly minced veal

¼ cup (60 ml) extra-virgin olive oil, divided

3 tablespoons (24 g) grated carrot or 1 small carrot, peeled and grated

2 cloves garlic, minced

1 teaspoon flour

3 tablespoons (45 ml) amontillado or oloroso sherry wine

3 to 4 cups (705 to 940 ml) chicken stock or water

In a small bowl, soak the hard bread in the milk.

Place 2 tablespoons (20 g) of the fried onion in a bowl. Add the egg, soaked bread, 1½ tablespoons (6 g) of parsley, and ¼ teaspoon each, salt and pepper. Combine thoroughly and then add the meat. Mix well with your hands for at least 3 minutes. Taste for salt.

Shape meatballs with your hands into round balls, from 12 to 18, about the size of a walnut or larger.

Put 1 tablespoon (15 ml) of the olive oil in a pan and add the remaining 10 tablespoons (100 g) onion, carrot, and garlic and fry for 5 minutes. Add the flour and fry for another 3 minutes, stirring constantly with a wooden spoon. Add the wine, raise the heat to high, and bring to a boil for 1 to 2 minutes. Add 3 cups (705 ml) of the stock and some parsley and cook over gentle heat, covered, for 10 minutes. Transfer to a blender and process into a sauce.

In a separate pan, heat the remaining olive oil and fry the meatballs, shaking the pan vigorously, until they turn golden on all sides. Pour the sauce over the meatballs. Cook over gentle heat, covered, for 10 to 15 minutes occasionally shaking the pan so that the meatballs cook evenly. Check for salt and pepper and add more of the stock if needed.

Serve with homemade diced fries or boiled rice. Garnish with some extra minced parsley.

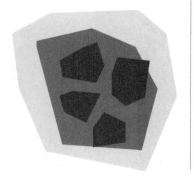

Stewed Round of Veal

SERVES 6

Round of veal is a very practical piece of meat to cook. It can be roasted, braised, or cooked in a salt crust in the oven. If using beef, increase the cooking time. It can be served a cold meat, too. Slice paper-thin and serve with an herb mayonnaise and a potato salad for a delicious summer dish that can be prepared ahead. It also freezes very well.

¼ cup (60 ml) extra-virgin olive oil

2½ pounds (1.2 kg) round of veal or other similar braising meat

2 large onions, diced (1 pound, or 450 g)

3 carrots, diced or grated (12 ounces, or 350 g)

½ green bell pepper, diced (3½ ounces, or 100 g)

3 cloves garlic, minced

1 stalk celery, diced

½ cup (120 ml) white wine

5½ to 6 cups (1.3 to 1.4 L) water

1 bouquet garni of fresh thyme, rosemary, bay leaf, and parsley or a pinch of dried herbs to taste (rosemary, thyme, oregano, and sage)

2½ teaspoons (15 g) salt, divided

Freshly ground pepper

Minced parsley

Diced fried potatoes, for serving

Cooked peas, carrots, cauliflower florets, brussels sprouts, potatoes, mushrooms, or parsnips, for serving

Heat the olive oil in a pot that can fit the meat and sear the veal on all sides until golden. (This will take approximately 5 minutes over high heat.) Set the meat aside.

Add the onions, carrots, bell pepper, garlic, and celery to the pot and sauté for 10 minutes over medium-low heat.

Add the wine, cook for 3 minutes, and return the meat to the pot.

Cover with the water and add the bouquet garni and 2 teaspoons (12 g) of the salt. Bring to a boil, lower the heat, and simmer for 30 minutes. Turn the meat over and cook for 10 to 15 minutes longer. The meat does not need to be totally cooked through; the center part will remain a little pink.

Remove the bouquet garni, transfer the sauce to a blender, and process until smooth. No need to strain. Return the sauce to the pot, and add the remaining ½ teaspoon (3 g) salt if needed, and season with the pepper.

Let the meat rest for 10 to 15 minutes, and then slice very thinly. Serve hot with the sauce and a garnish of minced parsley, fried potatoes, and the vegetables of your choice. Try to mix vegetable colors for a more attractive presentation.

NOTE

You can garnish your dish with a medley of steamed or boiled vegetables or a Vegetable Medley (page 76) without the sauce.

Iberian Pork Fillet

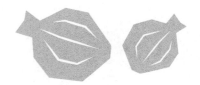

SERVES 4

Sherry is a traveling wine, one of the oldest in Europe. Three thousand years ago the Phoenicians, from present-day Lebanon, brought vine plants to a place in the south of the peninsula they called Xera. Sherry wines like oloroso and Pedro Ximenez, the sweetest of them all, are widely used in our cuisine. Alcohol disappears with cooking, but the wonderful aromas remain.

2/3 cup (50 g) raisins

1½ cups (355 ml) Pedro Ximénez sweet sherry wine

4 tablespoons (60 ml) extra-virgin olive oil, divided

2¼ pounds (1 kg) onions, thinly julienned

1 teaspoon salt

2 pork fillets (about 14 ounces, or 400 g, each)

½ cup (120 ml) Oloroso sherry wine

1 tablespoon (15 ml) sherry vinegar

Freshly ground pepper

1 teaspoon brown sugar

Flaky sea salt

In a small bowl, soak the raisins in the Pedro Ximénez wine for 2 hours.

Place 2 tablespoons (30 ml) of the olive oil in a pot with the onions and the salt and put over high heat; cook for 10 minutes, stirring with a wooden spoon. Then lower the heat, cover, and allow to cook gently for 10 to 15 minutes longer.

Heat 2 tablespoons (30 ml) olive oil in a pan and sear the pork fillets until golden on each side. This should take 10 minutes or more.

Add the onions and deglaze the pan juices with the Oloroso wine. Cook for 2 to 3 minutes, until evaporated. Add the Pedro Ximénez wine with the raisins. Cook for 5 minutes, turn the meat over, and cook 5 minutes longer.

Add the vinegar, pepper, and sugar and cook for 3 to 5 more minutes. Keep warm until it is time to serve.

Spoon the sauce onto a warm serving dish, slice the meat diagonally, place over the sauce, and sprinkle with some salt flakes. Accompany with steamed or sautéed spinach or bitter greens, such as kale, and a roasted potato per person.

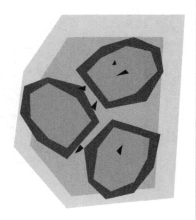

Chicken with Olives and Capers

SERVES 4

This recipe is from Andalucía in the south of Spain and is of a very old origin. The fish salting industry in Cádiz dates back more than three thousand years. Greeks and Romans widely used salted fish products as a seasoning in their cuisine. A condiment called garum, made from fermented salted fish, became the most expensive and sought-after ingredient in the Roman Empire. Following the path of our ancestors, you will find the combination of anchovies, sherry, olives, capers, and citrus fruit adds interest to the chicken.

1½ cups (150 g) pitted green olives

1½ tablespoons (12 g) capers in vinegar

3 tablespoons (45 ml) extra-virgin olive oil

4 to 6 chicken breasts (2¼ pounds, or 1 kg)

Salt and pepper

1 large onion or 2 small ones, finely minced

2 anchovies in olive oil, drained and minced

3 cloves garlic, minced, divided

½ cup (120 ml) oloroso or cream sherry wine

2½ cups (590 ml) good-quality chicken stock

1 bouquet garni with parsley stems, thyme, rosemary, and bay leaf

1 small piece orange peel

2/3 cup (180 ml) orange juice

1 tablespoon (15 ml) lemon juice

1 tablespoon (8 g) cornstarch

Fresh rosemary sprigs or minced parsley, for garnish

In a small bowl, soak the olives and capers in fresh water for at least 30 minutes to clean away the excess salt and vinegar. Rinse and strain.

Heat the olive oil in a pan over high heat. Add the chicken and sear on all sides until golden. Season with salt and pepper and set aside.

Add the minced onion to the pan and fry until slightly golden, 5 to 6 minutes, and then add the chopped anchovies and 2 of the minced garlic cloves and fry for 1 to 2 minutes longer.

Add the sherry wine and boil for 2 to 3 minutes to evaporate the alcohol.

Add the chicken stock, bouquet garni, orange peel, and a little salt. Simmer over low heat for about 10 minutes. Return the chicken to the pan, cover, and simmer gently for 8 to 10 minutes.

In a small bowl, combine the orange and lemon juices, add the cornstarch and stir to dissolve, then add to the pan. Add the remaining clove of minced garlic, the olives and capers, and a sprig of fresh rosemary. Turn the chicken over and cook for 5 minutes longer, or until the sauce thickens.

At this stage, the pan should be shaken and not stirred. Check for salt and pepper and serve immediately with boiled potatoes sprinkled with sweet pimentón (or paprika).

Chicken in Pepitoria

SERVES 4 TO 6

This is a traditional dish dating back to the Middle Ages and possibly of Arab origin. In our literature of the sixteenth and seventeenth centuries, it was very popular, as recorded by authors like Quevedo and Cervantes (in *Don Quixote*). Until very recently it was a classical wedding dish. Pheasant, turkey, geese, hen, lamb, or rabbit can be cooked pepitoria style. This dish is better the next day.

1 whole chicken (about 4½ pounds, or 2 kg), cut into 8 pieces, or the same amount chicken thighs or legs for a more even cooking (preferably organic and free range)

1 teaspoon salt, plus more for seasoning chicken

Freshly ground pepper

¼ cup (60 ml) extra-virgin olive oil, divided

1 cup (120 g) blanched raw almonds

3 cloves garlic

1 large onion, minced

1 bay leaf

A small piece of cinnamon or cassia bark (½ x 1 inch, or 1 x 2 cm)

½ cup (120 ml) dry white wine or fine sherry wine

3 to 4 cups (705 to 940 ml) chicken stock

2 hard-boiled eggs, peeled, whites and yolks separated, divided

A pinch of saffron threads or ¼ teaspoon saffron powder

1 whole clove

¼ teaspoon white peppercorns

1 sprig parsley

3 tablespoons (12 g) chopped parsley

Season the chicken pieces with salt and pepper.

Put the olive oil, almonds, and garlic cloves in a small pan. Fry over medium heat, stirring constantly, until they turn golden. Be careful, because they can easily burn. Set aside.

Add the almond–garlic oil to a larger pot and sauté the chicken pieces on all sides until golden. Set aside.

Add the minced onion, bay leaf, and cinnamon and sauté for 5 to 6 minutes, or until the onion turns transparent.

Add the wine, cook for 2 to 3 minutes, then return the chicken to the casserole and cover with the stock. Add 1 teaspoon salt.

Simmer for 20 to 30 minutes. Cooking time will depend on the size and quality of the chicken pieces. Free-range poultry might take longer to cook, so adjust the cooking liquid if necessary.

In a mortar, place the fried garlic cloves, half the fried almonds, egg yolks, saffron, clove, peppercorns, parsley sprig, and a pinch of salt. Mash to a fine paste. Ladle out 1 cup (235 ml) of the cooking liquid into the mortar with the garlic paste, and stir to dissolve. Add back into the casserole. This can also be done in a food processor.

Allow 5 to 10 more minutes cooking time for the sauce to thicken. Remove the bay leaf and cinnamon. Transfer the sauce to a food processor, process to a smooth sauce, and then strain the sauce before serving.

Serve the chicken hot, garnished with almonds, egg whites, and chopped parsley. Serve with boiled rice sautéed with pine nuts and raisins.

Hake in a Green Sauce

SERVES 4

In 1723, Mrs. Larrea wrote a letter to a friend about a new culinary discovery. Today, hake in a green sauce is possibly our most popular fish dish. Hake is highly valued for its delicacy and texture. Green sauce is an emulsion of olive oil, fish juices, and garlic, seasoned with parsley—very simple, but unique in its result. Be careful to cook the garlic gently so that it retains its color. This is the secret of this dish.

4 thick hake fillets cleaned, boned, and skinned (about 5½ ounces, or 150 g each)

Salt and freshly ground pepper

2½ tablespoons (37 ml) extra-virgin olive oil

2 cloves garlic, minced

¾ tablespoon (6 g) all-purpose flour

¼ cup (60 ml) dry white wine

2 cups (470 ml) fish stock

½ cup (30 g) minced fresh parsley

Lemon wedges, for garnish

Steamed potatoes, for serving

Fish stock

1 pound (450 g) fish bones and head

2 cloves garlic, minced

A few parsley stems

1 bay leaf

Pat dry the fish fillets with paper towels. Season with salt and pepper. Set aside.

In a small to medium-size, nonstick pan, add the olive oil and minced garlic. Place over gentle heat for 30 seconds to 1 minute so the garlic's scent comes out, then place the flour in a small colander and shake over the pan to distribute evenly. Stir with a wooden spoon and cook over very gentle heat for 2 minutes. The garlic must not color. Add the white wine and cook for 1 more minute, stirring constantly.

Add 1½ cups (355 ml) of the fish stock and cook for 8 to 10 more minutes over medium heat. You will have a thick sauce. If it is too thick, add a little more of the remaining stock. Check for salt and pepper.

NOTES

You may add peas, green asparagus, clams, or steamed potatoes for a more substantial main dish. If you do not have fish stock, add water or vegetable stock; the fish will release its flavor into the sauce.

If you prefer cornstarch as a thickener, dissolve 1 teaspoon cornstarch in ½ cup (120 ml) cold stock and add to the pan when the fish is half cooked. Shake the pan to prevent lumps.

Add the fish fillets to the pan and poach over very gentle heat for 3 to 4 minutes on each side. Cooking time will depend on the thickness of the fillets. Add the minced parsley, pour some sauce over the fish fillets to distribute the parsley evenly, and cook for 5 to 10 seconds more. Turn the heat off. The parsley should not overcook or it will turn dark brown.

Serve immediately with lemon wedges and steamed potatoes.

Fish stock: Place the bones in a pot, cover with water, and bring to a boil over high heat. Skim off the scum from the surface, add the garlic, parsley, and bay leaf, and lower the heat. Cook for 20 to 30 minutes. Pour through a sieve into a clean pot.

MERCADO JAMÓN IBÉRICO

Mercado
Jamón Ibérico

RACIONES COURSES

Jamón Ibérico - Bellota Platino	15,80 €
Jamón Ibérico - Bellota Oro	12,80 €
Jamón Ibérico - Calidad Plata	9,80 €
Jamón Serrano - Reserva 24 meses	6,80 €
Caña de Lomo - Bellota Platino	12,80 €
Lomo Ibérico - Bellota Oro	9,80 €
Taquitos Jamón - Ibérico de Bellota	8,80 €
Taquitos Jamón - Calidad Plata	6,80 €
Surtido Bellota - Calidad Oro	9,80 €
Lacón Ibérico - Calidad Oro	8,80 €
Tabla de Quesos - Surtido Calidad	12,80 €
Queso Puro - Oveja Salamanca	8,80 €
Surtido Lacón y Pastel Ibérico	8,80 €
Cecina de León - Calidad Oro	6,80 €

Mercado
Jamón Ibérico

DESAYUNOS BREAKFAST
SUPER OFERTA HASTA LAS 12 H.

Café, Té, Manzanilla, etc. con 2 piezas
de Molletes o Croissants rellenos de dulce o salado

Jamón Serrano
Lomo de Gijuelo
Jamón York
York y Queso
Chorizo Ibérico
Salchichón Ibérico
Pastel Ibérico
Crema de Queso y Anchoas
Crema de Queso y Sobrasada
Crema de Queso y Tomate
Crema de Queso y Cabrales
Crema de Queso y Chicharrones
Crema de Queso y Pavo
Jefe y Pimientos

2,65 €
CON ZUMO NATURAL
DE NARANJA

3,25 €

Vegetables and Salads

Because of our Mediterranean climate, we enjoy a great abundance and variety of fruit, vegetables and pulses of the highest quality. We are great lovers of de cuchara (spoon dishes) and vegetable dishes of which we have a great selection. Some of these easily become a main course when protein is added.

As for our famous cold soups such as gazpacho, they can be eaten as a tapa, a starter, during the meal or at the end of it as in some parts of Andalucía.

Stewed Lentils

SERVES 4

Lentil stew has been very popular since ancient times. In the Bible, Esau, son of Isaac, gave away his birthright—the right as the eldest son to all of his father's inheritance—to his brother Jacob for a plate of lentils.

1 pound (450 g) dried lentils

1 onion, diced

1 leek, white part only, cleaned and diced

2 carrots, peeled and sliced

1 stalk celery, diced

1 small turnip, diced

3 cloves garlic, sliced

1 large ripe tomato, peeled, seeded, and diced

1 meaty ham bone (optional)

2 chorizo sausages or other good-quality sausage thickly sliced (optional)

1 bay leaf

1 whole clove

Thyme

Parsley

10 to 12 cups (2.5 to 3 L) water

2 teaspoons (12 g) salt

2½ tablespoons (37 ml) extra-virgin olive oil

Put all the ingredients in a pot except the olive oil. Bring to a boil over high heat. Skim off the scum that rises to the surface and lower the heat. Cover and simmer for 1 hour. Check for salt and add more if needed.

Remove the red fat on the surface with the help of a spoon and discard. Taste the lentils; depending on their size they might need more water and more cooking time.

Turn the heat off and add some very good olive oil. It gives a wonderful aroma to your stew. Check for salt and pepper and serve hot with good sourdough bread or boiled rice.

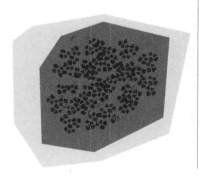

NOTES

I like lentils with lots of vegetables, so at home I cook lentils with fennel, kohlrabi, Swiss chard, parsnips, pumpkin, and celeriac. When done, I set part of it aside for myself. With the other half I add sliced chorizo sausage for the family, and cook for 10 to 15 minutes longer for the flavor to blend, so everyone is happy.

Leftover lentils make an excellent soup. Take 1 cup (250 g) lentil stew and add 2 to 3 cups (470 to 705 ml) milk, salt, and pepper, process in a food processor, and then heat and serve with fried croutons.

Potatoes Rioja Style

SERVES 4

A very popular country dish, this is the flagship of Riojan cuisine. It is simple and easy to feed large gatherings. Find a good chorizo sausage and extra-virgin olive oil. Break the potatoes instead of cutting them so that they will release their starch and thicken the sauce. Some like to add a very mature peeled, seeded, and minced tomato.

1 choricero dried pepper or 1 teaspoon sweet pimentón de la Vera (paprika)

6 starchy potatoes (2¾ pounds, or 1.3 kg)

3 chorizo sausages (½ pound, or 280 g)

2 tablespoons (30 ml) extra-virgin olive oil

1 green bell pepper, seeded and minced

1 large onion, minced

4 cloves garlic, minced

2 bay leaves

7 cups (1.6 L) water

Thyme

Salt

1 tablespoon (4 g) minced parsley, for garnish

Remove the seeds and stem from the dried pepper. Soak the pepper in warm water for 30 minutes to 1 hour. Remove the flesh and discard the peel.

Peel and cut the potatoes into big irregular chunks so more starch is released. Set aside in cold water. Slice the chorizo sausage.

Add the oil to a pan and fry the bell pepper, onion, and garlic for about 8 minutes, or until the onion is transparent and well cooked.

Add the sliced chorizo sausage and fry for 2 to 3 minutes, or until it releases the fat. Add the potatoes and bay leaves, stir for 2 minutes, then add the dried pepper or pimentón (paprika) and cover with the water. Season with salt. Bring the water to a boil and simmer for 30 to 40 minutes. The sauce should have a creamy consistency, thickened by the potato starch.

Check for salt, skim the fat off the stew, and remove the bay leaves. Serve hot, garnished with the parsley. A poached egg might be added for a more substantial meal.

NOTE

Mashed leftover potatoes over bread make a great tapa when grilled with cheese or with a fried egg on top.

Vegetable Stew

SERVES 4

Legend has it that this dish was served at the wedding of Arab princess Al Burun to Bagdad caliph Al Mamum (786-833), the greatest patron of science and philosophy in the history of Islam and the son of Harun Al Rashid, famous for the fairy tales of the Arabian Nights. In the time of Al Mamun lived the famous mathematician Al Khwarizmi, who is still celebrated to this day in the word algorithms, derived from his name.

1 teaspoon salt

1 eggplant, peeled and diced

¼ teaspoon salt

¼ cup (60 ml) extra-virgin olive oil

1 onion, diced

1 green bell pepper, seeded and diced

1 red bell pepper, seeded and diced

1 zucchini, unpeeled, diced

2 cups (380 g) diced pumpkin

6 ripe tomatoes, peeled, seeded, and diced, or 14 ounces (400 g) fried tomato sauce

2 cloves garlic, minced

½ teaspoon cumin seeds or powder (optional)

1 bouquet garni of bay leaf, thyme, parsley, and rosemary or dried herbs to your taste

½ teaspoon sugar

2 tablespoons (8 g) minced fresh parsley

Notes: You may also add a pinch of paprika, 1 teaspoon sweet sherry vinegar, or ½ cup (120 g) cooked chickpeas.

This is a great accompaniment for meat and fish. As a main course, add fried or poached eggs and serve with rice. It also makes a great sauce for pasta and can be eaten hot or cold.

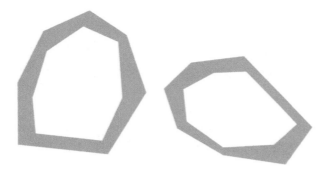

Add a little salt to the eggplant, mix with your hands, place over a colander, and let it "cry its bitterness out" for about 20 minutes. Discard the water.

In a small pan, heat some of the olive oil and sauté the vegetables separately, except the tomato, until all are finished. Remember to add a little oil with every vegetable. Each will take about 5 minutes over medium-high heat, except the pumpkin, which will take a little longer. When each batch is cooked, put in a larger pot.

Sauté the tomato and garlic until most of the liquid has evaporated. Add to the pot. Add the salt, cumin, bouquet garni, sugar, and parsley and simmer gently for 15 to 20 minutes for the flavors to blend. Check salt before serving. Remove the bouquet garni before serving.

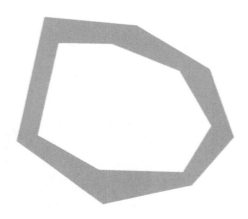

Country Potato Salad

SERVES 4

Potatoes, tomatoes, and peppers found their way to our Spanish kitchens after the discovery of the New World. Olive oil, vinegar, tuna fish, and onion have been in our diet for thousands of years. This is a real fusion dish and an extremely popular salad all over Spain. You can also dice the potatoes, if you prefer.

2¼ pounds (1 kg) new potatoes

Salt

7 ounces (200 g) minced scallion or onion

1 red bell pepper, seeded and diced

1 green bell pepper, seeded and diced

1 tomato, peeled, seeded, and diced

¾ cup (180 ml) extra-virgin olive oil

2 tablespoons (8 g) minced parsley, divided

¼ cup (60 ml) sherry vinegar

Wash the potatoes, but do not peel. Add to a pot with abundant salted water and cook for 20 to 25 minutes. Drain and set aside.

In a bowl, combine the scallion, peppers, tomato, salt, olive oil, 1 tablespoon (4 g) of the parsley and the vinegar. While the potatoes are still warm, peel, slice thickly, and place on a serving platter. Pour the vegetable dressing over while still warm. After 2 or 3 minutes mix carefully or shake so as not to break the potatoes.

Garnish with the remaining 1 tablespoon (4 g) parsley. Serve at room temperature.

NOTE

For a more substantial meal, you may add 3 hard-boiled eggs, peeled and cut into 4 slices each; some well-drained Pickled Tuna Fish (page 22); and some black olives.

Cold Vegetable Soup

SERVES 8

Originally made with bread, olive oil, vinegar, garlic, and salt mashed in a mortar, this soup is one of our most universal dishes. Considered by some a gastronomic masterpiece, it is the result of the wise handling of excellent local ingredients: the Mediterranean trilogy—wheat, olives, and grapes. This very refreshing soup can be a meal in itself or a tapa. There are hundreds of amazing varieties, four of which are below. Always remember to remove the germ of the garlic clove.

2¼ pounds (1 kg) peeled and seeded tomatoes

2 cloves garlic, peeled

3½ ounces (100 g) peeled and seeded cucumber (optional)

3½ ounces (100 g) red bell pepper

2 to 4 slices day-old bread

1 cup (235 ml) extra-virgin olive oil

3 to 4 tablespoons (45 to 60 ml) sherry vinegar

Salt

A pinch of ground cumin (optional)

Diced onion, cucumber, tomato, and green and red pepper, and cubed bread or croutons, for garnish

Process the vegetables and bread in a blender. Season to taste with olive oil, vinegar, salt, and cumin and serve ice cold with the garnishes on the side.

Variations

If you substitute one-third of the tomatoes for watermelon you will have a delicious watermelon gazpacho to be served with diced pickled herring and/or diced avocado.

To make cherry or strawberry gazpacho, substitute 15 to 20 percent of the tomatoes for fruit.

To make beetroot gazpacho, add a small cooked beet or half of a large one to the recipe. These gazpachos might need a little more salt to balance the sweetness.

To make Pipirrana: For a different soup, dice all the ingredients, except the bread, into small pieces. Add garnishes, season, and combine. Season to taste and add a few ice cubes to chill. Serve cold. This is called "pipirrana." It is even more refreshing with mint leaves.

Vegetable Medley

SERVES 6

This is a spring dish, when all new vegetables are in season. Use as many as you want. It can be eaten with a poached egg on top for a more substantial dish. If you are a vegetarian, discard the ham in this recipe and add a couple of minced garlic cloves when sautéing the onion. It will be just as good.

6 artichokes

1 pound (450 g) Swiss chard (only the stems, keep the leaves for another use)

7 ounces (200 g) green beans or sweet peas

4 tender young carrots

½ head cauliflower, cut into bite-size florets

1 pound (450 g) fresh sweet peas or 2 cups (260 g) frozen

1 bunch green asparagus

Salt and freshly ground pepper

2 cups (470 ml) vegetable stock from cooking the vegetables

4 tablespoons (60 ml) extra-virgin olive oil

3 tender new onions, white part only, finely minced (about 1½ cups, or 240 g)

2½ ounces (75 g) Iberian ham, minced

1 tablespoon (8 g) cornstarch

Minced parsley

Clean, peel, and cut the vegetables. Cut flat green beans in half lengthways and then into 2 or 3 parts.

Cook the vegetables separately in boiling salted water until almost done: artichokes and Swiss chard, 6 to 8 minutes; green beans, 3 to 4 minutes; carrots, 3 to 4 minutes; cauliflower, 3 minutes; peas, 1 minute; and asparagus, 1 minute. It all depends on the freshness of the vegetable and the size of the cut.

Drain, cool, and place all vegetables in a casserole. Measure out 2 cups (470 ml) of the boiling liquid and set aside.

In a small skillet, heat the olive oil and sauté the onions over low heat until transparent, 6 to 8 minutes, then add the ham and stir fry for 1 minute longer. Add 1½ cups (355 ml) of the vegetable cooking liquid and raise the heat.

Dissolve the cornstarch in the remaining ½ cup (120 ml) cooking liquid and add to the skillet. Boil for 1 minute.

Pour the sauce over the vegetables, and cook 3 to 5 minutes, covered. Shake the casserole, rather than stirring, so that the vegetables do not break. Check the seasoning. Add more vegetable liquid if needed.

Garnish with the minced parsley and serve hot.

Cheese-Stuffed Piquillo Peppers

SERVES 6

Manchego cheese comes from the plains of central Spain, the area known as Castilla-La Mancha. It is our most popular pressed cheese and is made with milk from Manchego ewes. This area is also famous for its saffron, considered to be the best in the world. Piquillo peppers are a specialty from Navarra, in the North of Spain. For this recipe we will need a cured or aged cheese that does not melt too easily.

24 Piquillo peppers (3 cans or jars)

14 ounces (400 g) cured Manchego cheese

½ cup (80 g) fried onion

½ cup (122 g) tomato sauce

1½ cups (356 ml) vegetable stock

A pinch of saffron threads

2 tablespoons (8 g) minced parsley, divided

1½ tablespoons (12 g) pine nuts or chopped almonds

Salt and pepper

Preheat oven to 425ºF (220ºC or gas mark 7).

Drain peppers and reserve the liquid.

Remove the crust from the cheese and slice in triangles of about ⅛ inch (35 mm). Fill all of the peppers with cheese, being careful that no cheese sticks out of the pepper. You may need to adapt the size of the cheese pieces to the size of the pepper. Place stuffed peppers on an oven-proof serving platter.

Put the fried onion, tomato sauce, stock, pepper liquid, saffron, and half of the parsley in a blender and season to taste with salt and pepper. Process until very fine and pour over the peppers. Sprinkle some pine nuts or chopped almonds on top. Place in a hot oven for 20 to 30 minutes.

Garnish with parsley and serve as a main dish with some rice and sautéed spinach on the side. This dish can also be served as a tapa.

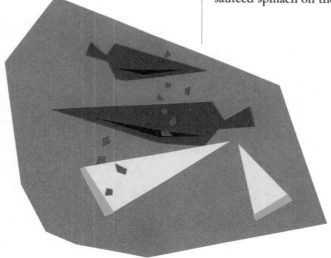

May Your Life be Sweet

"May your life be sweet," or "Live sweetly," are Sephardic greetings, as well as an expression of thanks to someone who offers you sweets.

In Spain, every region, city, village, and even saints are celebrated with their own specific sweet. During the festivities of the Madrid patron saint, San Isidro, rosquillas (a kind of donut), can be found in every pastry shop. Turrón is a Christmas sweet made with sugar, honey, and almonds. Buñuelos de Viento or wind puffs and Huesos de Santo or holy bones are the popular sweets eaten during All Saints Day. We also have a very large variety of sweets made with eggs. Especially famous are the Yemas de Santa Teresa of Avila (egg yolks and sugar). The Suspiros are made with the remaining egg white, sugar, and almonds. Volumes could be written on Spanish sweets, so I hope you enjoy this selection.

Santiago Almond Cake

SERVES 6

This cake celebrates Saint James, patron saint of Spain. According to legend, the Apostle Saint James the Elder is buried in the Galician city of Santiago de Compostela. For more than a thousand years people from all over the world have walked the pilgrimage route to this marvelous city to visit the saint's tomb in the cathedral and obtain the saint's blessings.

4 large organic eggs

A pinch of salt

Grated zest of 1 organic orange

Grated zest of 1 organic lemon

1¼ cups (250 g) granulated sugar

2 cups (250 g) almond meal

Confectioners' sugar, for serving

Preheat the oven to 425°F (220°C, or gas mark 7).

Line a 10-inch (24 cm) cake pan with parchment paper, as this is a very sticky cake.

In a bowl, beat the eggs, add the salt, orange zest, lemon zest, and granulated sugar and mix well. Then add the almond meal and stir to combine.

Pour the mixture into the pan and bake for 15 to 20 minutes. We like it slightly soft in the middle but cook to your taste.

Cool, transfer to a serving platter, and sprinkle with confectioners' sugar. In Spain it is easily recognizable because the Saint James cross is stenciled on the cake.

NOTE

I like to mix in different nuts, such as coconut flakes and almonds, and also stuff it with lemon curd and red berries. Occasionally, I like to add ¼ cup (30 g) dried cranberries, which give a nice acidity to the cake.

Chocolate and Churros (Fritters)

SERVES 4, OR 12 TO 24 PIECES, DEPENDING ON SIZE

Chocolaterias, the public establishments in sixteenth-century Mexico where tchocolatl was drunk, are still very popular in Spain today. Churros, wheat-dough fritters, are the best creation to be dipped into thick hot chocolate. Talk about modern fusion food! This is a great example of a lasting combination of ingredients from both worlds, as sugar arrived in Spain with the Arabs. When vanilla and chocolate met with wheat, olive oil, and sugar, a sweet revolution was started!

Chocolate

2 cups (470 ml) milk

7 ounces (200 g) dark chocolate (70% cocoa), broken into pieces

Granulated sugar

Churros

1 cup plus 1 tablespoon (250 ml) water

1 teaspoon salt

1 tablespoon (15 ml) olive oil

1 cup (120 g) all-purpose flour, loosely packed, sifted

1 egg white (optional)

2½ to 3 cups (590 to 705 ml) olive oil, for frying

¾ cup (100 g) confectioners' sugar

To make the chocolate: Pour the milk into a pan, bring to a boil over medium-high heat, add the chocolate, stir for 1 to 2 minutes, and remove from the heat. Keep stirring so the chocolate will dissolve. Add granulated sugar to taste.

To make the churros: Place the water, salt, and olive oil in a pan and bring to a boil. Add the flour and stir until the dough comes away from the sides of the pan. Cool for a few minutes.

Add the egg white and mix with a whisk until all is blended and you obtain a soft, but consistent, dough. (Egg white is not necessary but it is a little trick to make things easier.) Place the dough in a piping bag with a ridged star tip or better, in a churrera (a churro pipe).

Heat the olive oil in a deep pot to 350ºF (180ºC). Pipe pieces of dough over the hot oil and fry for 50 seconds to 1 minute or until they are golden on both sides. Drain on paper towels. Depending on the length and shape of your churros you can obtain from 12 to 24 pieces.

Sprinkle with confectioners' sugar and serve with the hot chocolate. Do not forget to have the sugar bowl on the side to dip the churros in.

> **NOTE**
>
> You may need to slightly alter the amount of liquid you use because flours vary from one brand to another. Be careful when frying churros, because they can explode for several reasons: if the dough is too wet, if it has air bubbles, or if the oil temperature is not hot enough.

Baked Apples with Custard

SERVES 4

Both cinnamon and vanilla are very important spices in our desserts. Apple and cinnamon are a classic, especially when it comes to helping an upset stomach. Vanilla bean seeds give custard a special quality. Leftover beans are washed, dried, and kept in sugar to flavor it. If beans are not available, use vanilla extract.

4 apples, Reineta variety or any other tart cooking apple

4 cinnamon sticks

1 tablespoon (15 ml) lemon juice

1 tablespoon (15 g) brown sugar

1 tablespoon (14 g) butter or (15 ml) extra-virgin olive oil

2½ cups (590 ml) milk, divided

1 vanilla pod or vanilla extract

½ lemon peel

4 tablespoons (50 g) granulated sugar

½ tablespoon (4 g) cornstarch

2 whole organic eggs

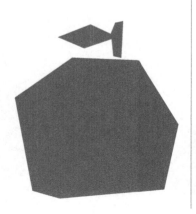

Preheat the oven to 350ºF (180ºC, or gas mark 4).

Wash and core the apples. Put the apples on a baking tray. Place a cinnamon stick inside each apple. Evenly distribute the lemon juice, brown sugar, and butter inside the apples. Bake for 20 to 30 minutes. Baking time depends on the size of the apples and your personal taste. There should be a little juice left at the bottom of the baking tray. Substitute sugar for honey or jam if you prefer.

To make the custard: Set aside ¼ cup (60 ml) of the milk. Put the remaining 2¼ cups (530 ml) milk in a saucepan. Slice the vanilla bean in half lengthwise, scrape the vanilla beans into the milk, and leave the bean in the saucepan. Add the lemon peel and granulated sugar. Bring to a boil, turn the heat off, cover the pan, and infuse for 15 minutes.

In a bowl, dissolve the cornstarch in the reserved milk, add the eggs, and mix well. Carefully add the flavored milk to the egg mixture, stirring constantly. Return the eggs and milk to the saucepan, place over medium-low heat, and keep stirring in the same direction for 12 to 13 minutes. It must not boil.

When the cream thickens, turn the heat off and keep stirring. Strain the cream into a bowl and place in another bowl filled with ice water, stirring occasionally so as not to form a skin. Serve in a sauceboat with the baked apples.

NOTE

The custard requires patience and care, but the result is highly rewarding.

Meringue Milk Ice Cream

SERVES 6

This is a light, delicious, and easy way to make ice cream based on a traditional Spanish summer drink. You can eat it both ways: as an ice cream or as a granita or slushy. It has an addictive flavor and is also very refreshing.

4 cups (940 ml) whole milk

1 cinnamon stick

1 lemon peel (preferably organic)

1 cup (120 g) confectioners' sugar, divided

3 egg whites

A pinch of salt

Ground cinnamon, for garnish

Add the milk, cinnamon stick, and lemon peel to a medium-size pot and bring to a boil over medium-low heat so that the milk will not overflow. Cook for 2 to 3 minutes stirring constantly. Add ¾ cup (90 g) of the sugar and stir to dissolve. Let the milk infuse and cool with the spices in it. You will obtain an aromatic milk.

Strain the milk into a clean bowl and put in the freezer, stirring occasionally.

When the milk is almost frozen, beat the egg whites and salt in a bowl with an electric mixer, until fluffy. Add the remaining ¼ cup (30 g) sugar and beat for another 2 minutes to obtain a stiff meringue.

Add the meringue to the almost frozen milk and mix well. Keep in the freezer, stirring occasionally, until totally frozen.

Serve in a glass or cup and sprinkle with ground cinnamon on top. This dessert can be totally frozen or served like a slushy to drink with a straw.

NOTE

This dessert is delicious with fresh fruit salad, with the Santiago Almond Cake (page 84) and even with Torrijas (page 96). Here in Spain it is also served with coffee granita.

Orange Confit

SERVES 4

The "food of the gods," the cacahuaquahitl, or cocoa plant is shrouded in legend. Quetzalcoatl, the Feathered Snake, a major deity in ancient Mexico and the god of agriculture, medicine, astronomy, and fine arts, gave this plant to his beloved people as a present. The Aztecs used cocoa nibs as coinage, and this explains the popular saying "money grows on trees." When we were little and wanted money, our parents used to say, "Children, do you think money grows on trees?" It certainly did in Aztec times!

Orange Confit

4 organic oranges

1 organic lemon

1½ cups (355 ml) water

1 cup plus 1 tablespoon (212 g) sugar

Chocolate cream

½ cup (120 ml) water

1½ tablespoons (18 g) sugar

7 ounces (200 g) 70% cocoa dark chocolate, chopped

½ cup (120 ml) mild and sweet extra-virgin olive oil

4 generous slices sweet bread, brioche, or any bread you like

¼ teaspoon flaky sea salt

To make the orange confit: Peel the oranges and lemon with a tomato peeler or a sharp knife, using only the colored part. Slice thinly into julienne strips. Peel the oranges until no white is left. Set aside. Cut the lemon in half and squeeze the juice from one of the halves. Set aside.

In a pot, blanch the strips in boiling water for 2 minutes and then discard the water.

Add the 1½ cups (355 ml) clean water and the sugar to the pot and bring to a boil. Simmer gently, uncovered, for 20 minutes. Add the lemon juice, cook for 1 minute longer. Set aside.

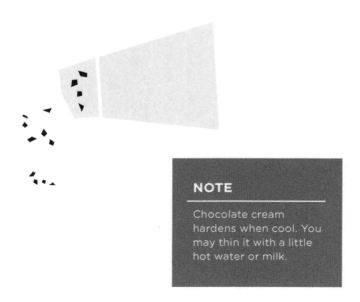

NOTE

Chocolate cream hardens when cool. You may thin it with a little hot water or milk.

To make the chocolate cream: Put the water and sugar in a small pan and bring to a boil; when the sugar has dissolved, add the chocolate. Remove from the heat and stir until the chocolate has melted.

Add the olive oil little by little, in a thin stream, always stirring in the same direction until all is well combined. You will obtain a shiny chocolate cream.

Toast the bread and cover generously with the chocolate cream and 1 or 2 salt flakes. Place an orange on the side and drizzle with the candied peel and syrup. The bread will soak up some of the syrup. It's delicious!

Serve the remaining chocolate cream in a bowl to be passed around.

Torrijas

SERVES 4

Torrijas, an Easter Lent dessert, is loved all over Europe and in America is known as French toast. But nowhere has it reached the fame it enjoys in Spain. It is no longer just served during the Easter season and now appears all year-round on top restaurant menus. At home we only cook them in season, and keep them in the fridge for people to help themselves. Accompany with berries, ice cream, custard, or whipped cream. Even bakeries make a special bread just for torrijas.

eight to ten ½-inch or (1.5 cm) thick slices day-old bread

2 to 2½ cups (470 to 590 ml) milk

1 cinnamon stick

Lemon peel

1½ tablespoons (18 g) sugar, plus more for sprinkling

Extra-virgin olive oil, for frying

3 eggs

Ground cinnamon, for serving

For the honey sauce:

¾ cup (180 ml) water

½ cup (160 g) honey

Place the bread in a deep baking pan that fits all.

In a saucepan, boil the milk with the cinnamon stick, lemon peel, and sugar for 2 to 3 minutes. Lower the heat so the milk will not overflow. Discard the cinnamon and lemon peel and carefully pour the milk over the bread into the pan.

Let soak for 20 minutes or more. The bread must go soft and absorb all the milk. It helps to soak the bread edges first in the very hot milk.

Put the olive oil in a pan and heat. Meanwhile, beat the eggs in a bowl with a mixer for 1 minute. Dip the bread slices into the egg and fry in the very hot olive oil until golden on both sides. Fry all of the bread, drain on paper towels, and transfer to a large platter that can fit all. Sprinkle with a mix of sugar and ground cinnamon.

To make the honey sauce: Bring the water to a boil in a small pan, add the honey, and stir to dissolve. Carefully pour the honey sauce over the torrijas and keep in the fridge; they will keep for 3 to 4 days, if you are lucky. Normally, they tend to disappear very quickly!

NOTE

We like torrijas with a honey sauce. They can also be soaked in sweet wine, fruit juice, or seasoned light syrup. Eat anytime or as a dessert. To give them a different shape, carmelize the top part of the torrija with the sugar and a kitchen blowtorch, then place a scoop of ice cream on top.

Menus

Stewed Lentils
Stuffed Eggs
Meringue Milk Ice Cream

Vegetables Cocas
Homemade Meatballs
Baked Apples with Custard

Grilled Green Asparagus
Shrimp Fideuá
Orange Confit

Shrimp in Garlic Sauce
Vegetable Stew
Potato Omelet
Baked Apples with Custard

Roasted Vegetables
Country Potato Salad
Pickled Tuna Fish
Torrijas

Gazpacho
Valencian Paella
Santiago Almond Cake with Fresh Fruit

Country Potato Salad
Stewed Round of Veal
Orange Confit

Stuffed Eggs
Cheese-Stuffed Piquillo Peppers
Meringue Milk Ice Cream with Fresh Fruit

Vegetable Medley
Chicken Saffron Almond Stew
Meringue Milk Ice Cream with Fresh Fruit

Potatoes Rioja Style
Hake in Green Sauce
Torrijas

Salad My Way
Iberian Pork Fillet
Orange Confit

Mushrooms with Garlic Parsley Sauce
   in the Style of la Rioja
Hake in Green Sauce
Santiago Almond Cake with
   Meringue Milk Ice Cream

Bread with Olive Oil, Tomato,
   and Iberian Ham
Grilled Green Asparagus
Potato Omelet
Baked Apples with Custard

Vegetable Medley
Hake in Green Sauce
Torrijas

Watermelon Gazpacho
Country Potato Salad
Stuffed Eggs
Santiago Almond Cake with
   Lemon Curd and Berries

Vegetable Cocas
Chicken with Olives and Capers
Baked Apples with Custard

Vegetable Stew
Homemade Meatballs
Torrijas

Grilled Green Asparagus
Salad my Way with Pickled Tuna Fish
Santiago Almond Cake

Tapas menu:

Bread Olive Oil, Tomato, and Iberian Ham
Mushrooms with Garlic Parsley Sauce
   in the Style of la Rioja
Potato Omelet
Salad My Way
Roasted Vegetables on Toast
Pickled Tuna Fish
Iberian Pork Fillet on Toast
Chocolate and Churros (Fritters)

Outdoor menu:

Stuffed Eggs
Mushrooms with Garlic Parsley Sauce
   in the Style of la Rioja
Grilled Green Asparagus
Potatoes Rioja Style
Santiago Almond Cake and
   Ice Cream

Pickled Tuna Fish on Toast
Roasted Vegetable Salad
Valencian Paella
Orange Confit

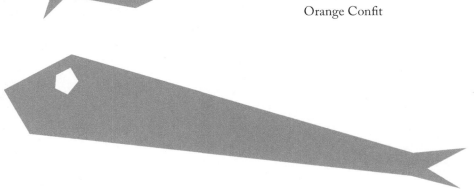

Add Your Own
Spanish Recipes

Recipe

Recipe

Recipe

Recipe

Recipe

Recipe

Recipe

Recipe

Recipe

Recipe

_____
_____
_____
_____
_____
_____
_____
_____
_____
_____
_____
_____
_____
_____
_____
_____
_____
_____
_____
_____
_____
_____
_____
_____

Recipe

Recipe

Recipe

Recipe

Recipe

Recipe

Recipe

Recipe

Recipe

Recipe

Acknowledgments

Thanks to my parents, Clara María and Lino, and to my grandmother, Primi for a wonderful gastronomic education, a limitless generosity, and so many important teachings. Thanks to the light my brother left. Thanks to my sisters, nieces, and nephews that we may keep enjoying ourselves round a table!

Thanks to my students and clients of all these years for their interest, enthusiasm and appreciation!

About the Author

Chef, teacher, caterer, author, and food promoter
for the past fifteen years, Gabriella Llamas has run
her own business, La Huerta del Emperador (the
Emperor's Orchard), which is devoted to artisanal,
traditional Spanish food, made with the best
ingredients. With individual cooking classes, cooking
parties, olive oil and wine tastings, and food tours,
she shares the secrets of timeless, traditional Spanish
cuisine with clients and friends alike. She feels very
fortunate to learn so much from them.

Index